GUIDE TO
ARMS
AND
ARMOUR

Andrew Kershaw

Illustrated by Dick Eastland

Designed by Vanessa Clarke

A Piccolo Explorer Book
Pan Books · London and Sydney

Below: A Japanese samurai warrior fires his bamboo bow. The samurai warriors were the ruling class in Japan from the 11th century until the late 19th century.

Contents

About This Book

Arms and armour have played an important part in shaping history. Throughout the ages, people have used weapons for defending themselves and for conquering others. Wars have always caused destruction and suffering, but for thousands of years war has been going on somewhere in the world.

This book provides a fascinating insight into the development of weapons, armour and tactics of warfare through the ages. It traces their history from the early warriors and the first metal weapons through to the introduction of firearms and the nuclear weapons of today.

The First Warriors

For hunting, attacking others, or defence, prehistoric people had to arm themselves with weapons. They found that by chipping hard stones – like flint – into shape they could make heads for axes, arrows and spears.

The discovery of metals, more than 6000 years ago, led to better and stronger weapons. Copper was the first metal to be used. The Sumerians of the Middle East made many of their weapons of copper. They had powerful armies of infantry (foot soldiers) and charioteers armed with spears.

Around 3000 BC copper was hardened by adding tin to produce bronze. The early Egyptians used bronze weapons. But, in about 1200 BC, they learned, probably from the Hittites, to make iron weapons. The Egyptians also had horse-drawn chariots and armies of up to 20,000 soldiers. The soldiers carried spears, maces and strange swords called *khepeshes*. Meanwhile, in northern Mesopotamia, a fierce race called the Assyrians had developed a powerful and well-equipped army. They learned to use iron around 1300 BC. With these improved weapons and huge armies they built a mighty empire.

▶ **Egyptian foot-soldiers** did not wear armour, but protected themselves with large shields.

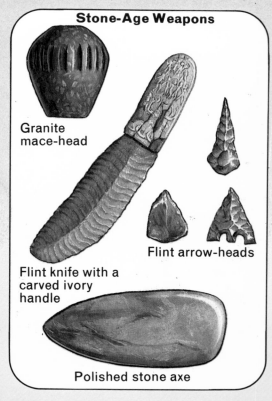

Stone-Age Weapons

Granite mace-head

Flint knife with a carved ivory handle

Flint arrow-heads

Polished stone axe

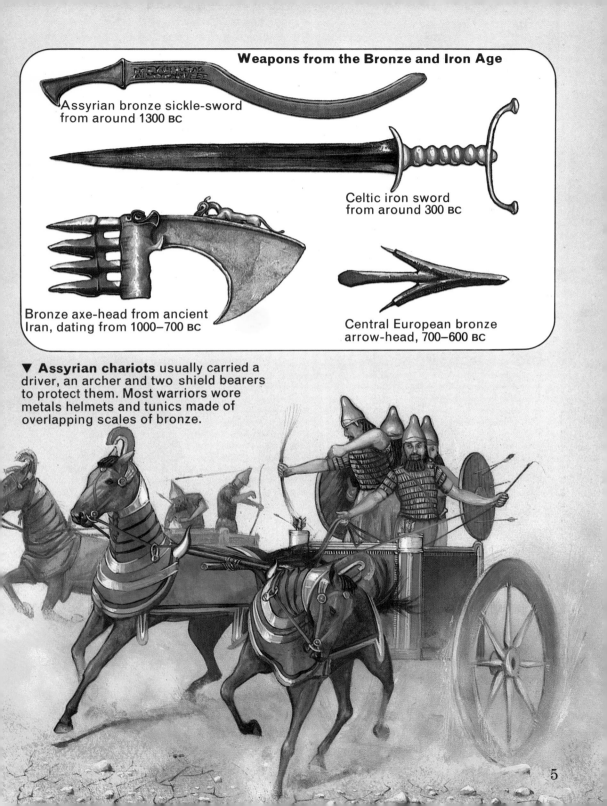

Weapons from the Bronze and Iron Age

Assyrian bronze sickle-sword from around 1300 BC

Celtic iron sword from around 300 BC

Bronze axe-head from ancient Iran, dating from 1000–700 BC

Central European bronze arrow-head, 700–600 BC

▼ **Assyrian chariots** usually carried a driver, an archer and two shield bearers to protect them. Most warriors wore metals helmets and tunics made of overlapping scales of bronze.

5

Greek hoplite wearing Corinthian helmet

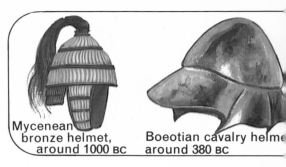

Mycenean bronze helmet, around 1000 BC

Boeotian cavalry helme around 380 BC

Greeks and Romans

The Greek infantry, called *hoplites*, were the first to make wide use of body armour (see left). They fought in close formations called *phalanxes*, carrying swords, shields and 6-metre pikes. Supported by light infantry wielding slings, javelins and bows, the well-trained phalanxes crushed their enemies. They would advance steadily behind a wall of shields bristling with spears.

The phalanx was improved under Alexander the Great, who conquered the Assyrians and built a 'second Greek empire' between 336 and 323 BC. His empire collapsed after he died, leaving Rome and Carthage to fight for control.

At the battle of Zama in 202 BC, Rome's well organized army finally beat the armies of Hannibal of Carthage. From there the Romans went on to conquer most of Europe and the Middle East. The army was divided into *legions*, each with 5000 to 6000 men. The main weapons of the *legionary* (see right) were a short stabbing sword, or *gladius* and a long spear, or *pilum*.

Etruscan
helmet, 100 BC

Roman cavalry
helmet,
2nd century

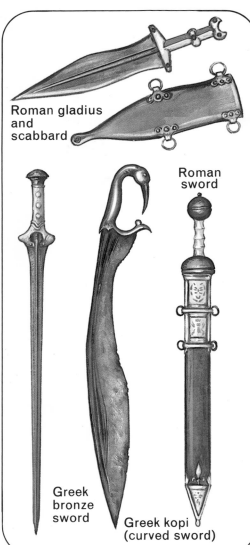

Roman gladius
and
scabbard

Roman
sword

Greek
bronze
sword

Greek kopi
(curved sword)

Roman
legionary

Mail Armour

Mail was used in Roman times but it was very expensive to make. Even by the Middle Ages it had still not completely replaced *scale armour*. However, in the Dark Ages, many Viking warriors wore mail tunics. Some of these Vikings settled in France and became the Normans. The Normans wore a coat of mail called a *hauberk* with a hood called a *coif*. Some knights were covered head-to-toe in about 18 kilogrammes of mail armour. The last famous mail-clad warriors were the Crusaders. The weight of their armour often made them too slow to catch the lightly-armoured Saracens.

▶ **Vikings** wore coats of mail and metal helmets. They carried round wooden shields, axes and swords.

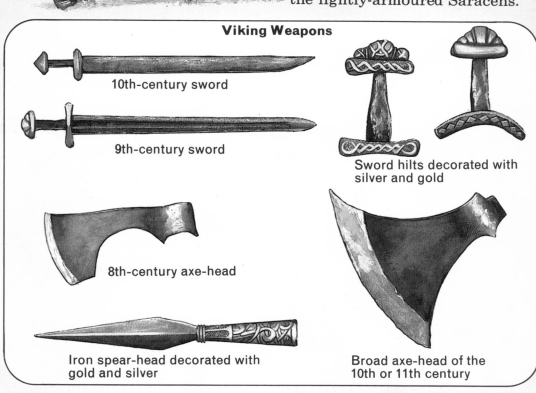

Viking Weapons

10th-century sword

9th-century sword

Sword hilts decorated with silver and gold

8th-century axe-head

Iron spear-head decorated with gold and silver

Broad axe-head of the 10th or 11th century

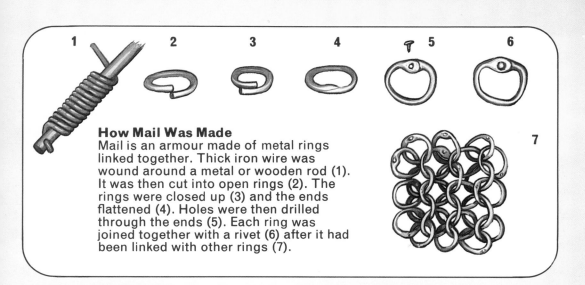

How Mail Was Made

Mail is an armour made of metal rings linked together. Thick iron wire was wound around a metal or wooden rod (1). It was then cut into open rings (2). The rings were closed up (3) and the ends flattened (4). Holes were then drilled through the ends (5). Each ring was joined together with a rivet (6) after it had been linked with other rings (7).

▼ Saxon armour Many Saxons wore mail tunics and metal helmets.

▼ Norman armour The horse-riding Normans wore helmets with distinctive *nasals*.

▼ Crusaders wore long white coats called *surcoats* over their mail armour.

▼ Saracens wore little armour. Some wore mail helmets completely covering the face.

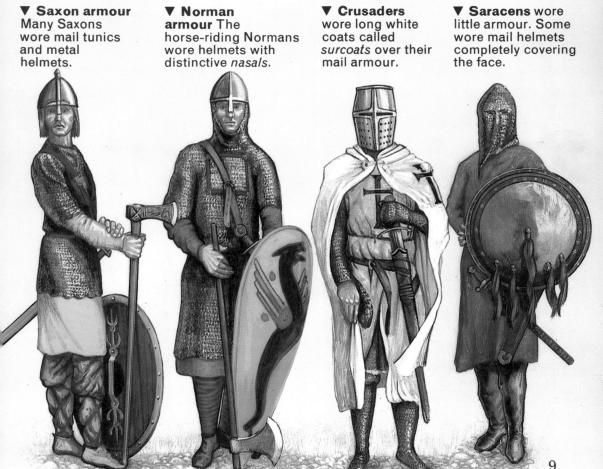

Bows and Arrows

The bow is one of the earliest weapons. The Assyrians were well-known for their archers (see page 5). The Mongol hordes of Asia and the American Indians have also been experts with the short bow, using it both in war and hunting.

In Europe, however, powerful crossbows gradually took over from the short bows during the Middle Ages. As stronger materials were used to make bows, so it became harder to pull back the cord. From the 14th century crossbowmen often used a belt hook, or a winder called a *cranequin*, to arm their bolts.

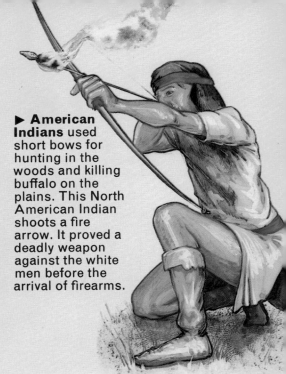

▶ **American Indians** used short bows for hunting in the woods and killing buffalo on the plains. This North American Indian shoots a fire arrow. It proved a deadly weapon against the white men before the arrival of firearms.

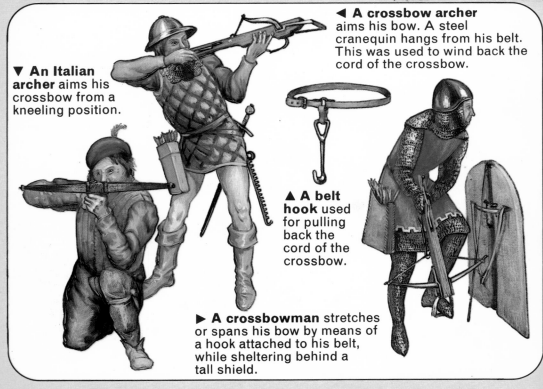

◀ **A crossbow archer** aims his bow. A steel cranequin hangs from his belt. This was used to wind back the cord of the crossbow.

▼ **An Italian archer** aims his crossbow from a kneeling position.

▲ **A belt hook** used for pulling back the cord of the crossbow.

▶ **A crossbowman** stretches or spans his bow by means of a hook attached to his belt, while sheltering behind a tall shield.

Much quicker than the crossbow was the longbow used with metre-long, steel-tipped arrows. It was also just as deadly over 300 to 350 metres. The English adopted this weapon from the Welsh. They made it famous as a killer of the heavily armed, mounted French knights at the battles of Crécy (1346), Poitiers (1356) and Agincourt (1415). In fact, the English kept the longbow for almost 200 years. This was long after firearms, like those used by the French, had outdated it.

▼ **Longbow archers** prepare to fire their steel-tipped arrows.

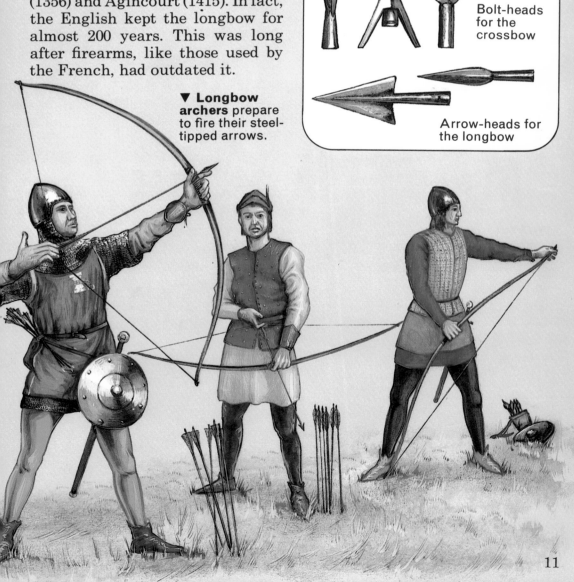

Longbow arrow

Crossbow bolt

Bolt-heads for the crossbow

Arrow-heads for the longbow

11

Plate Armour

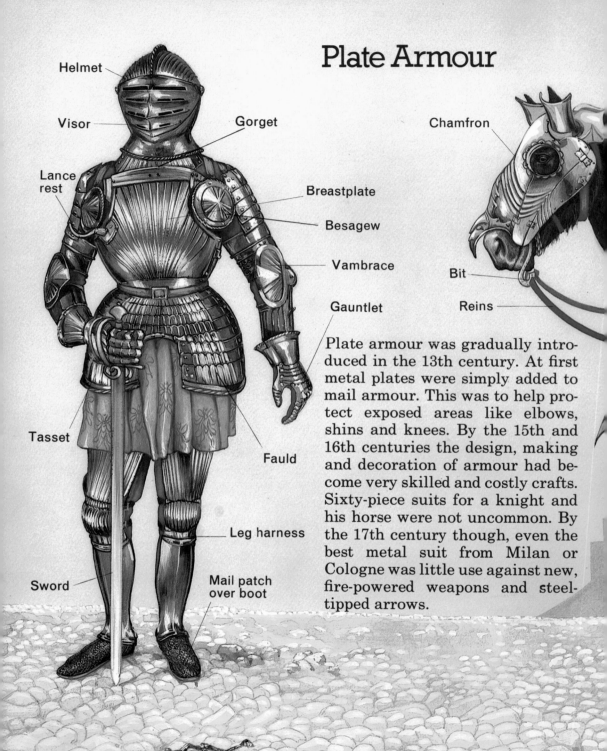

Helmet

Visor

Gorget

Lance rest

Breastplate

Besagew

Vambrace

Chamfron

Bit

Reins

Gauntlet

Tasset

Fauld

Leg harness

Sword

Mail patch over boot

Plate armour was gradually introduced in the 13th century. At first metal plates were simply added to mail armour. This was to help protect exposed areas like elbows, shins and knees. By the 15th and 16th centuries the design, making and decoration of armour had become very skilled and costly crafts. Sixty-piece suits for a knight and his horse were not uncommon. By the 17th century though, even the best metal suit from Milan or Cologne was little use against new, fire-powered weapons and steel-tipped arrows.

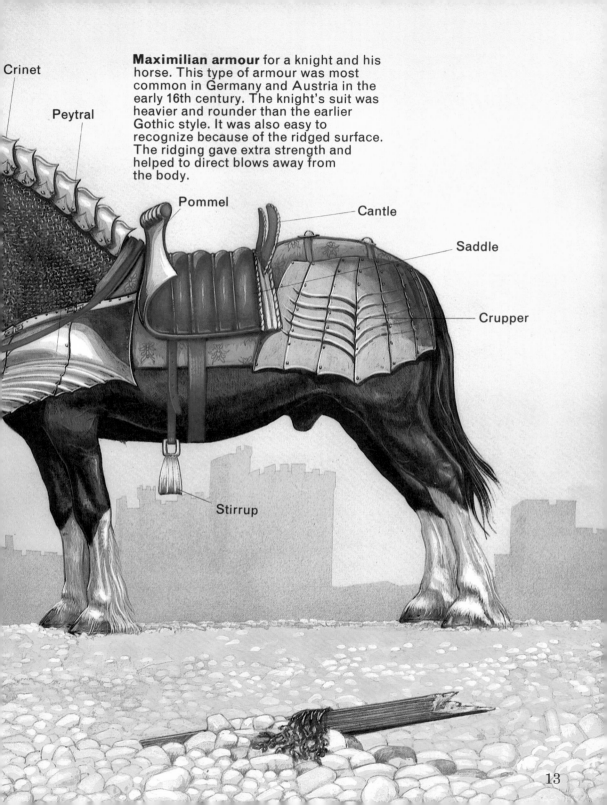

Crinet

Peytral

Maximilian armour for a knight and his horse. This type of armour was most common in Germany and Austria in the early 16th century. The knight's suit was heavier and rounder than the earlier Gothic style. It was also easy to recognize because of the ridged surface. The ridging gave extra strength and helped to direct blows away from the body.

Pommel

Cantle

Saddle

Crupper

Stirrup

13

Pikes, Swords and Daggers

▲ **Swords** changed with fashion and to meet new needs. From left to right: a 16th-century two-handed sword; a 17th-century rapier; a 15th-century cut and thrust sword; and a 19th-century sword.

Swords of all sorts have long been battlefield weapons. Most of the early swords were broad and long for slashing. During the Middle Ages the point of the sword became more important and special thrusting swords were made.

Daggers were also popular edged weapons. But, after the 17th century, they were largely replaced by bayonets. Many types of pole-arms and maces also proved useful against armour.

◄ **A pikeman** in decorative Italian dress from the early 17th century (below left) prepares for the cavalry charge with his pike and sword. The pike was made of ash and was about five metres long. The pikeman's job was to protect the musketeer when he was reloading his musket

▼ **Daggers, Maces and Polearms**
1. Plug bayonet
2. Rondel dagger
3. Holbein dagger
4 and 5. Left-handed daggers, popular in the 17th century
6. Morning star mace
7. Flanged mace
8. War hammer
9. Spiked staff

10. Halberd
11. Boar spear
12. Poleaxe
13. Bill

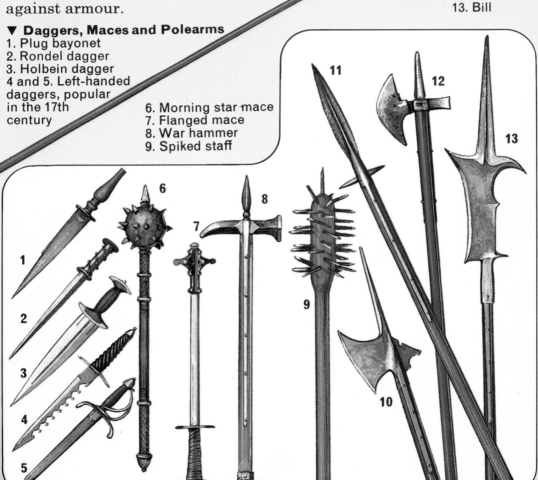

15

Early Firearms

Just as steel-tipped arrows could fell an armoured knight, so cannon (first used at the siege of Metz in 1324) could destroy his castle. At first *artillery* was often a greater danger to its user than its target. Early handguns were also both inaccurate and slow. By the 17th century both types of firearms were plentiful and deadly. Shot-firing, muzzle-loading muskets, such as *matchlocks* and *flintlocks*, appeared first. The *rifled* barrels and explosive, breech-loading cartridges were introduced in the early 1800s. These improvements made both handguns and rifles accurate, fast and deadly weapons. Soon cannon barrels were also rifled for accuracy and power. Pistols and 'repeater' rifles became common in the 19th century. Then there came the machine guns – Gatlings and Maxims – and warfare was about to undergo one of its most violent changes.

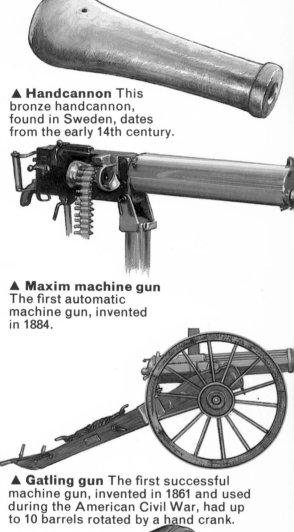

▲ **Handcannon** This bronze handcannon, found in Sweden, dates from the early 14th century.

▲ **Maxim machine gun** The first automatic machine gun, invented in 1884.

▲ **Gatling gun** The first successful machine gun, invented in 1861 and used during the American Civil War, had up to 10 barrels rotated by a hand crank.

▼ **A naval cannon** used on board ship in sea battles during the 19th century.

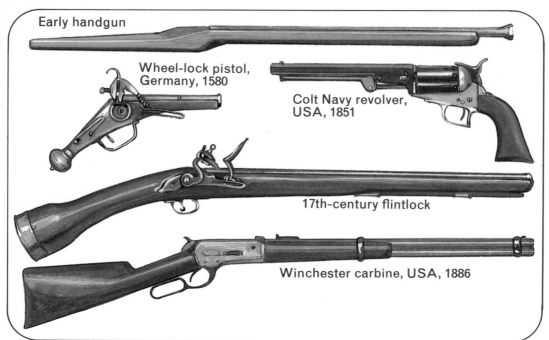

Early handgun

Wheel-lock pistol,
Germany, 1580

Colt Navy revolver,
USA, 1851

17th-century flintlock

Winchester carbine, USA, 1886

▼ **A breech-loading cannon** of the
15th century. This cast bronze siege
weapon fired solid balls which could
knock down the thickest castle walls.
But early cannon were not always
accurate and sometimes exploded,
killing their loaders.

Modern Guns

Modern firearms are designed for accuracy, 'killing power' and the fastest possible rate of fire. Once only heavy machine guns, like the Vickers and Lewis, could do all these things. Today, there are lighter hand-held sub-machine guns and automatic rifles which can do the same job. Automatic pistols, like the Mauser and Colt, became popular at the turn of the century.

▶ **Anti-aircraft gun** This modern powerful anti-aircraft gun, with two long thin barrels, can destroy attacking aircraft from the ground.

With the coming of fighter aircraft, machine guns and cannons took to the air. Some, like the modern Vulcan rotary cannon, can pump out thousands of shells a minute with enough power to pierce any armour. Anti-aircraft guns are used to combat warplanes.

On the battlefield, modern weapons can fire shells over scores of kilometres with pinpoint accuracy. With grenade-launchers and bazookas, even the ordinary soldier now has the firepower of a small-scale artillery.

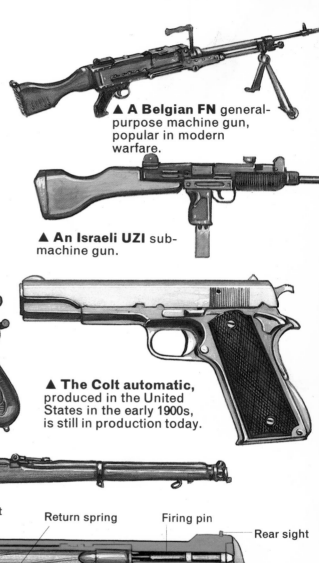

▲ **A Belgian FN** general-purpose machine gun, popular in modern warfare.

▲ **An Israeli UZI** sub-machine gun.

▲ **The Mauser,** a classic German pistol, was first made in 1896 and is still used today. It was the first successful automatic pistol to be mass-produced.

▲ **The Colt automatic,** produced in the United States in the early 1900s, is still in production today.

▲ **The Lee-Enfield,** a popular British rifle of World Wars I and II, is still used today.

▶ **The Browning** self-loading pistol of 1968 carries 13 9-mm shells in a magazine in the butt.

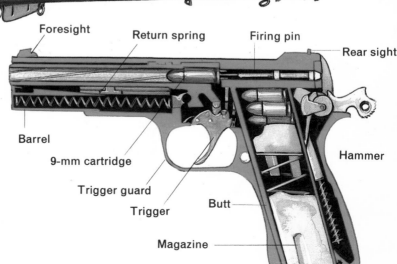

Foresight

Return spring

Firing pin

Rear sight

Barrel

9-mm cartridge

Trigger guard

Trigger

Hammer

Butt

Magazine

Tanks

Armoured vehicles carrying heavy guns on caterpillar tracks first appeared in 1915. Although they were slow and often unreliable, they made light of barbed wire and machine guns. Tanks also helped the British and French to break the trench stalemate of the Western Front during World War I.

By 1939, and the start of World War II, the Germans in particular had fast, hard-hitting machines in their Panzers, Panthers and Tigers. But it was the Russians, Americans and British who were to win the tank war in Europe. They did this by sheer weight of numbers of T-34s, Shermans and Churchills.

Tanks have since got faster, been better armed and armoured. Nowadays only massive air power could stop a modern tank army on the move.

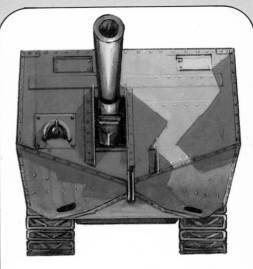

▲ **The Schneider,** a French tank of World War I, had a crew of six, with a 25-mm armour protection and a 75-mm gun.

▼ **The Mark IV tank** was used by the British during World War I. It had two large guns and four Lewis machine guns. The caterpillar tracks made it easier to cross the many obstacles on the battlefields.

Sherman tank An American tank of World War II, with a four-man crew, 81-mm armour protection and a 76-mm gun.

Tiger tank A German tank of World War II, with a five-man crew, 100-mm armour protection and a 88-mm gun.

▼ **Self-propelled guns** look very similar to tanks. This modern Swedish 105-mm gun is mounted on to a tank chassis.

The Missile Age

The first modern missiles were Germany's V-1 ('doodlebug') and V-2 rockets of World War II. From them, in under 30 years, bigger, faster and more powerful rockets carrying nuclear or biological bombs have been built. These include long-range *ballistic missiles*, tactical battlefield missiles, air-launched *cruise missiles* and even orbiting space missiles. The bomb, or warhead, is carried in the nose of the missile. Some missiles can carry several warheads. At a moment's notice, missiles can be launched against pin-point, pre-programmed targets all round the globe.

▲ **The 'Honest John' missile** is a ground-to-ground artillery missile used by the army. It is a dangerous weapon with a range of about 20 kilometres.

▲ **The Carl Gustav rocket launcher** is a Swedish-made weapon for use against tanks. It will fire high explosives, smoke and flares.

▼ **A nuclear submarine** launches a missile from under the water. These submarines can roam underwater for several weeks at a time. The side of this submarine is cut away to show the missile launch tubes. It carries a row of eight on each side.

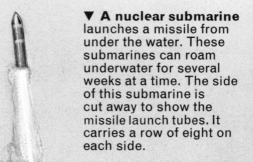

Glossary

Artillery Large firearms mounted on wheels or a fixed base, such as cannon, mortars and howitzers.

Ballistic missiles Any missiles which are thrown, fired or projected.

Cavalry Any mounted troops. Originally the mounts were horses, but soldiers using armoured cars, tanks or other vehicles are also called cavalry.

Cruise missile A small jet-powered rocket usually carrying a nuclear warhead which is launched from a flying aircraft and piloted to its target by a small computer.

Flintlock Firearms with a device which produced a spark by striking flint to steel when the trigger was pulled.

Infantry Foot-soldiers. Depending on the type of armour and weapons they use, infantry may be called *light* or *heavy*.

Matchlock A firearm with a slow-burning match which touched gunpowder in a small pan when the trigger was pulled.

Musket A firearm in which the inside of the barrel is smooth, not *rifled*.

Nasal A bar projecting from the rim of a helmet to protect the face (see page 9).

Phalanx A solid formation of soldiers which advances with pikes pointing forward.

Polearm Any weapon attached to a pole, such as a pike, poleaxe, bill, halberd or partizan.

Rifling Spiral grooves around the inside of a firearm's barrel which cause the bullet to spin in flight. This spinning causes the bullet to travel further, faster and more accurately to its target.

Scale armour was made by attaching overlapping plates of metal to a leather tunic.

Surcoat A long tunic worn over armour for decoration, recognition or to keep off the sun.

Wheel-lock A firearm using a steel wheel and a piece of pyrites to strike a spark.

Index

Books to Read

Arms and Armour by Frederick Wilkinson (A. & C. Black)

War and Weapons by the staff of the National Army Museum, London (Sampson Low)

Arms and Armour by Frederick Wilkinson (Macdonald Educational)

Warriors and Weapons 3000 BC to AD 1700 by Niels M. Saxtorph (Blandford)

Tanks and other Armoured Fighting Vehicles 1900–18 by B. T. White (Blandford)

Tanks and other Armoured Fighting Vehicles of the Blitzkrieg Era 1939–41 by B. T. White (Blandford)

Exploring War and Weapons by Brian Williams (Pan)

Weapons of the Ancient World by Rivka Gonen (Cassell)